The Unknown God

A Look At The Apostle Paul's Transit In Athens

MONICA DENNIS-JONES

The
Unknown
God

Elohim spoke to Moses, "I am Yahweh. I appeared to Abraham, Isaac, and Jacob as El Shadday, but I didn't make myself known to them by my name Yahweh.

Exodus 6:2-3 (NOG)

ISBN-13: 978-1532743788

ISBN-10: 1532743785

Due to the dynamic nature of the Internet, Web addresses and links contained in this book may have changed since publication and may no longer be valid.

DEDICATION

To YHWH, the greatest Author of all time, for allowing me the awesome privilege of being called His child;

To my father, Mr. Joubert Dennis, affectionately called Brother Gee (Deceased), my mother, Mrs. Ionie Rosetta Dennis (Sister Gee), who brought me up in the fear and admonition of the Lord Jesus Christ

My family, Franklyn Kennedy Jones, Franklyn Kennedy Jones, Jr., and Fereia Kendra Jones whom I love dearly, my siblings, Yvette Dennis-Robinson, Veronica Dennis, Denval Dennis, Claudia Dennis-Walton, my cousins Pauline Ewan and Nadine Ewan-Wisdom

My Caribbean Gospel Radio FM (CGR FM) family across the world, that they may walk in the ways of the Lord all their days and experience His manifold blessings in their lives.

CONTENTS

ACKNOWLEDGMENTS

I am deeply grateful to God, YHWH, for blessing me with a wonderful Radio Ministry, Caribbean Gospel Radio Faith Ministry (CGR FM). The family members of this ministry have been very supportive of my calling. Thanks Pastor Wayne Smith for filling my broadcaster's seat so I could complete this leg of the journey.

My amazing children, Kennedy and Kendra Jones, as well as my extended family have been a great source of encouragement along the journey. Thank you for allowing me time away from you to research and write. I love you dearly.

Thanks to the wonderful staff at Newburgh Theological Seminary and School of Bible Theology, Indiana, especially Dr. Les Liebengood who advised me along the way. For that, I am extremely grateful.

My deepest gratitude to my friend, Angela Burns for the encouragement provided and for the hours spent editing my work. It was a great comfort and relief to know that you were willing to come on board as my editor. Thank you. Minister Marcia S. Watson-Sayers, thank you for lending your expertise on printing matters.

1 INTRODUCTION

The book of Acts is a record of the works and doings of the disciples of Jesus Christ. Jesus, the Messiah had already been crucified, buried, risen and ascended to heaven but the disciples had a work to do. That work was to take the good news of salvation to the world.

According to Gene R. Simowitz, "The book of Acts is an exhilarating book about fascinating people, dramatic events and great truths. ... It is the only unfinished book of the Bible, practically speaking...because we are still writing the history of the Church day by day." [1]

Acts gives us a condensed history of the early Church. Through its pages, we get to see the eyewitness accounts of the way The Gospel miraculously spread to Rome from Jerusalem. It records the events surrounding the Day of Pentecost and the ripple effect of that great event. During this time, the followers of Jesus Christ witnessed to the Jews in Jerusalem. We see Peter at the center of the Church at that time, but later on, another man by the name of Saul came on the scene.

This Saul was from Tarsus in Cilicia. The website Sacred-Destinations describes Tarsus in the following way:

Tarsus was the most important commercial port in the province of Cilicia since 2300 BC. A few decades before Christ, the Romans granted her the

---

[1] Gene R. Simowitz, *Evangelism: A Road* Less *Traveled* (Xulon Press, 2012), 277

status of a free city with the privileges such a title entailed.

Mark Antony and Cleopatra lived in Tarsus in the 1st century BC.

The Apostle Paul was born in Tarsus and seemed to be proud of his birthplace. In Jerusalem, as he was being arrested, Saint Paul told the tribune: "I am a Jew and a citizen of the well-known city of Tarsus in Cilicia.[2]

This Saul, being a Jew, a zealous young Pharisee, persecuted the followers of Jesus Christ. In an effort to stop the spread of the Christian faith, he hunted down the Christians, imprisoning and killing them. On one of these journeys to persecute the church, he had a strange encounter with Jesus. It was a life changing experience, so much so that he started to preach in the synagogues that Jesus is the Son of God. During this encounter popularly known as **"the Damascus Road experience"** the Lord called him by his Jewish name "Saul" which means "desired'. The Lord also called him "Saul" when He

[2] Tarsus, Turkey, http://www.sacred-destinations.com/turkey/tarsus (accessed February 7, 2015).

instructed the prophets and teachers at Antioch to separate to Him Barnabas and Saul for the work to which He had called them.

The first time we see Saul being called Paul was while he was in Cyprus preaching along with Barnabas. We learn that he did not have a name change, as is widely believed. Saul was also called Paul. The writer of the book of Acts records "Then Saul, (who also is called Paul), filled with the Holy Ghost, set his eyes on him"[3] Paul was his Roman name, meaning "little or small."

By the time we get to chapter 17 of this fascinating book we see the Apostle Paul on his way to Thessalonica. After much unrest there, he was sent off to Berea, along with Silas, to save his life. Things did not change much for them in Berea because as soon as the Jews whom they left behind in Thessalonica, heard about the good work they

---

[3] Acts 13:9 (King James Version)

were doing, they tried their very best to cause a commotion in Paul's life again. This time, in order to save Paul's life, he was taken to Athens, the place that would later become known for Paul's most famous speech of all time.

What was this place, Athens like? What was the daily life of the inhabitants of such a city? What was the culture of the Athenians? We will follow Paul's journey in an effort to see what we can discover about this city.

This city had philosophers, various religions and not to mention the many gods that they believed in and worshiped. They had some strange doctrinal points as well. Paul, discovering this, set out on a path to declare the only true and living God, YHWH (Yahweh) to the men and women of the city of Athens.

2 PAUL'S TRANSIT IN ATHENS

(Acts 17:16)

The Apostle Paul arrived in Athens with the hope of being joined at a later time by Silas and Timothy, his companions who were left behind in Berea. Seemingly, he took a tour of this city and found something that really disturbed him. What was that? He found that there were a lot of idols in the city of Athens. Now, Paul being a Jew was not used to all of this. The Jews, from the beginning of

time, had been warned of God, YHWH:

> Thou shalt have no other gods before me.
> Thou shalt not make unto thee any graven image, or any likeness of anything that is in heaven above, or that is in the earth beneath, or that is in the water under the earth.
> Thou shalt not bow down thyself to them, nor serve them: for I the Lord thy God am a jealous God, visiting the iniquity of the fathers upon the children unto the third and fourth generation of them that hate me;[4]

Seeing this level of idolatry, Paul's spirit was

disturbed. Accounts given by heathen writers tell us that

there were more idols in Athens than there were men in all

Greece. Petronius, the believed author of the Roman novel,

Satyricon, is quoted as saying, in regards to Athens, "It

was easier to find a god than a man there." [5]

---

[4] Ex 20: 3-5

[5] http://biblehub.com/commentaries/acts/17-16.htm (Accessed February 17, 2015)

The Athenians were very welcoming to the gods and deities of other nations. Whatever deity was recommended to them, they admitted them and allowed them a temple and an altar. The arts and superstitions of these other nations were readily accepted as well, hence the erection of the many idols that Paul encountered.

After this encounter, Paul took to the synagogue where he tried to reason with both the Jews and the devout persons. The Jews were those who belonged to the Jewish nation whether by birth, origin or religion. The devout persons, as described by Jesse Lyman Hurlbut in *The Story of the Christian Church* were different from the Jews. "The devout...were Gentiles who ceased to worship idols, and attended the synagogue, but had not undergone circumcision, did not undertake to observe the minute requirements of Jewish rules, and were not counted among Jews, though friendly to them."[6]

This reasoning or "dispute" as the King James version of the Bible calls it, is from the Greek word **dialegomai** meaning to converse, discourse with one, argue or discuss. It also means, to think different things with one's self, mingle thought with thought; to ponder or revolve in mind. Paul had some conversation or argument with the Jews as well as the Gentile worshipers on the matter of the idol worship in their city. It was prevalent and was not hidden. Were they involved in such idol worship? Or, did it not matter to them that the people around them were worshiping other gods instead of the true God, YHWH?

Paul did not only converse with the "church folks" because it is recorded that he also took this concern to the market place. Now, this market place was a place of assembly of the people so, Paul approached them every day about the matter of their idol worship.

[6] Jesse Lyman Hurlbut, *The Story of the Christian Church.* (Zondervan Publishing House, 1970), 18

There was grave concern on Paul's part, because he saw so many pagan temples and altars in Athens. Sacrifices and offerings were being made to these lifeless deities yet the name of YHWH, neither Jesus, the son of YHWH was not mentioned. Did the Athenians not know about Him? Did the Jews keep their God a secret? He was seemingly never mentioned among the many gods of Athens, as we will discover. Could the inscription to the "unknown god" which Paul later discovered, be that of the God of the Jews?

The demon sacrifices and offerings that Paul stumbled upon in Athens really troubled him. He was concerned for the brethren, for by allowing this to take place they were in fact having fellowship with the powers of darkness. Sadly, the brethren in Athens were being deceived by the devil.

Paul was left with one resolve and that was to teach the Athenians about his God. He was not afraid to declare Him.

He was in fact a bold man in declaring the resurrection of Jesus Christ, so much so, that he drew the attention of some famed Greek philosophers. This did not scare Paul. He saw an opportunity to declare YHWH to a city full of idol worshipers, and he did so.

While in transition in Athens, awaiting Silas and Timothy, the Apostle Paul, even in the face of opposition, defended the Christian faith. Never flinching once nor being concerned as to the possible fate that he could face for defying their many gods, Paul preached his immortal sermon in famous Athens on Mars Hill.

3 A LOOK AT ANCIENT GREECE

Let's Explore Athens

Athens was not just one of the many cities in Ancient Greece. It was the greatest city there; home to some of the best leaders, writers, philosophers and artists in history. The level of intelligence residing in this city was powerful.

The city of Athens was strategically situated in the most advanced culture in the ancient world at this time. Athens ran a democracy. As a matter of fact, it was the first to do so. Foreigners were allowed to reside there alongside its citizens. The citizens were afforded the privilege of having a say on how the city should be run, but the foreigners didn't have a say. They couldn't vote at all. Slaves and women were also not allowed to vote.

In her writings on The Ancient Greeks, Rosemary Rees tells us how this democracy worked in Athens:

> Each citizen of Athens was a member of the assembly. The assembly met once a week. Any citizen could speak at assembly meetings. A council of 500 citizens was chosen each year by drawing lots. The council decided what was to be discussed at assemblies. Council members looked after the management of the city. A lottery also was used to choose the board of ten generals who were to be responsible for the protection of Athens against invaders. [1]

This assembly which was known as the ekklesia, was put in place to ensure that no one individual held too much power in Athens. This ekklesia made all the important

---

[1] Rosemary Rees, *Understanding People In The Past; The Ancient Greeks* (Crystal Lake, IL: Heinemann Library, 1997), 11

decisions as it concerned the city and according to Peter Connolly, in his book, Ancient Greece, "This met once every nine days or so and at least 6000 people had to attend. Women and slaves were not allowed into the ekklesia." [2] Prior to this, it was tyrants that ruled Athens.

The members of the assembly had the opportunity to remove anyone they disliked. Examining the democracy of Athens, Rosemary Rees states that "Once a year, members of the assembly had the chance to throw out anyone they disliked. Each member scratched a name on a piece of pottery...the person with the most votes against him was sent away for ten years."[3]

The ekklesia or assembly had a strange and unique way to get people to attend its meetings. Prior to the start of each meeting, officials would take a long rope that was

---

[2] Peter Connolly, *Ancient Greece* (Oxford University Press, 2001) 40

[3] Rosemary Rees, *Understanding People In The Past; The Ancient Greeks* (Crystal Lake, IL: Heinemann Library, 1997), 11

covered with red powder and tie it across the end of the market place. They then used the rope to drive the people toward the assembly platform. If anyone outside the assembly was found with red marks on his clothes, he could face punishment, because he should have been at the assembly platform.

Citizens of Athens took their turn once a year at being council members, judges and officials. The duty of the judge was to give verdicts on disputes and quarrels between citizens. They did this by voting with bronze discs. The person was considered innocent if most of the bronze discs used, had solid knobs. A verdict of guilty would be determined, if most of the discs used had hollow knobs.

The Athenian system of law courts was very well developed. They possessed a strong sense of fair play. If you were a lawbreaker, chances are you would be tried in

Athens' Supreme Court the Heliaia or Heliaea where the hearings took place outdoors under the sun. However, if someone committed murder, they would usually be tried by a separate council, known as the Areopagus.

Punishment in Athens took on different forms. In his book Ancient Greece, Peter Connelly explains:

> Prison was not the most common way of punishing wrong-doers in Athens. Criminals might be fined or have their property taken, or they could be exiled (forced to leave Athens). Murderers were usually executed. Slaves were whipped or branded for crimes. The only people put in prison for crimes were foreigners, or criminals awaiting execution. [4]

Although Athens was a democracy, it is said that strong personalities could still influence the ekklesia.

Life in Athens seemed to be pretty interesting. The marine industry was thriving and the city boasted a large fleet of trading ships. From April to September when the

---

[4] Peter Connolly, *Ancient Greece* (Oxford University Press, 2001) 44

weather was good, traders sailed. Athens was a trading state producing olives for oil and grapes for wine.

As a means of transportation, carts were sometimes used to carry luggage and passengers. Being pulled by horses, these carts transported goods. Baskets, carried on the backs of donkeys were sometimes used to carry goods. Those who were of the richer class rode in chariots.

As we explore Athens in the Apostle Paul's day, we find that this city was so powerful that the surrounding cities paid Athens to protect them from enemies. Because of their power, the Athenians had money to buy statues, beautiful buildings and paintings. They spent time reading, writing and even discussing ideas.

Athens took pride in beautiful buildings. One such building was the Acropolis. The word **Acropolis** in Greek literally means **"the highest point of the town."** This building was between 60 and 70 meters above the city on

Athens' highest hill. It measured 200 meters from east to west and 150 meters from north to south. It housed temples and other buildings there are well. Greek history tells us that;

> Besides a fort and a place of royal residence, the Acropolis functioned as a place of worship for the Goddess of fertility and nature, and for her companion male god Erechtheus … The Acropolis of Athens had its own underground water supply in the form of a deep well, dug at the north end of the rock, which could be used by the defenders during a siege.[5]

The Acropolis housed the Parthenon, temple of Athena Parthenos; The Propylaea, entrance way; The Bronze statue of Athena; Temple of Nike (Victory) and Pinakotheke, picture gallery. Another building housed there was The Erectheum. It was named after Erectheus, Athens' first king who was also a legendary hero. The Erectheum was really two temples, each of which

---

[5] "History of the Acropolis" http://ancient-greece.org/history/acropolis.html (accessed February 24, 2015).

contained tombs and sacred sites of different gods or heroes.

The Parthenon was a beautiful building. Built mostly from white marble from Mount Pentelicon, the general design was traditional, bearing a similarity to temples all over ancient Greece. The Parthenon was known as one of the most beautiful and famous buildings in the world due to its size, the details of its design and the superb sculptures which decorated it.

The People and Their Culture

On this visit to Athens, the Apostle Paul clearly saw that Athenians lived different lives depending on their social status. Men also lived very different lives from women. The wealthy men were the only ones who could truly enjoy the freedom and cultural life offered by the city. The women were expected to spend most of their time taking care of the house and the children. The poor and the rich lifestyles were also different and the slaves lived a different life from the free citizens. They had no freedom at all as they were constantly at the command of their masters.

Boys and girls were brought up at home until about age seven. They were told stories, such as Aesop's fables and rhymes by their mothers. Some of these stories are still being told today. Dolls and balls were items they would play with and some would be privileged to ride in toy chariots. After age seven the girls would help out around the house.

In spite of the difference in lifestyles, every boy, except those who were really poor were afforded the privilege of going to school when they got to the age of seven years. A slave caretaker, also known as a paidotribes or pedagogue, bore the responsibility of taking the boys to and from school, reviewing their work and maintaining a disciplined behavior in them. The teachers held school in their house where they taught the boys.

From age twelve, the most important part of a boy's schooling was exercise and physical education. When it came to exercising, the boys would take off their clothes and sprinkle themselves with dust or fine sand to prevent chills. Exercise included wrestling, gymnastics and sports such as throwing the javelin and discus, running and jumping. These events would take place in an open space called the gymnasium and were done in an effort to make them strong enough to fight. Parents who could not afford to send their boys to school would have them work on the land. Most Athenian boys went to work with their fathers and grandfathers and learned a craft, while some studied with a philosopher.

Explaining what the Daily life in Athens was like, Peter Connolly in his book Ancient Greece says "Boys learned to read and write and to do arithmetic. They learned history from Greek writers. And as they got older they learned to sing and play the lyre or flute."[6]

The girls led a different lifestyle as Peter Connolly explains: "Athenian girls did not go to school. However, in richer families they might have a tutor at home, who would teach them to read and write, and to play music and sing. Athenian girls did not take part in sports and exercises like the boys."[7] The girls from the neighboring Greek city of Spartan, however, exercised in public which was very shocking to the Athenians who did not.

When Paul visited Athens it wasn't likely that he would have encountered many young men at the age of

---

[6] Peter Connolly, *Ancient Greece* (Oxford University Press, 2001) 15

[7] Ibid., 16

eighteen years because at that age, they would have already finished their schooling and would have entered the military school for training for a two-year period. It was mandatory for the boys to do so because all Athenian men had to serve in the army whenever there was war.

The people of Athens did not have large families. They valued boys, way more than girls in that culture. For a girl to be married, she needed a dowry. She had to pay money to the bridegroom's family. Marriages were arranged by the fathers of the couple as Rosemary Rees explains in her writings, The Ancient Greeks:

> People felt it was their duty to get married and have children. Marriages were arranged by the fathers of the couple. The girl and boy did not have to love each other. Sometimes they did not meet until the wedding ceremony. All that mattered was that the wife-to-be would make a good mother. The girl's family arranged for her to give a dowry which was usually a sum of money, to the boy she was to

[8] Rosemary Rees, *Understanding People In The Past; The Ancient Greeks* (Crystal Lake, IL: Heinemann Library, 1997), 14

marry. Girls were usually married when they were about fifteen years old. Boys were normally older.[8]

Life in Athens was vibrant, so no doubt weddings were being held while Apostle Paul was in transit there. In this culture, they held their weddings at home. Peter Connolly gives us a sneak preview into this part of the culture;

> An Athenian girl married at the age of 14 or 15. She had no say about who she married. Marriages were arranged between the groom and the father of the bride.
>
> On the day before the wedding, the bride made a sacrifice to one of the wedding gods: Hera, Zeus, Artemis or Apollo. Her favorite dolls, clothes and toys were burnt on the altar as an offering to the god. After this ceremony the girl took a bridal bath. At his house, the groom also bathed on the eve of his wedding.[9]

The morning of the wedding was spent preparing a wedding feast at the bride's house. The bride would be dressed in her best clothes, with a veil crowned with a

---

[9] Peter Connolly, *Ancient Greece* (Oxford University Press, 2001) 22

wreath of leaves. It was traditional that in the afternoon the bridegroom would go to the bride's house along with his family and the best man. After the sacrifice was made to the gods everyone sat down to the feast. As was the custom, the men were not allowed to sit with the women. The new couple was then presented with gifts from the guests in attendance.

As the night approached, the bride's father would present her to the bridegroom. They would then ride in a chariot or a cart to the groom's house where his family would welcome her, the new bride, while the guests shower her with nuts and figs.

Athenians were very superstitious people. As the couple entered the house, the wedding guests would sing very loudly in an effort to ward off evil spirits they thought were likely to be present. They would then kneel by the fire and say prayers. On the following day, the bride's family would visit them for a feast, bringing along presents as well.

Being married was not a security, because a husband could divorce his wife any time he pleased. If he divorced her though, he would have to give back her dowry, the money she paid his family. In this culture, the husband was also allowed to marry his wife to someone else without her consent. It was a bit tougher on the wives because if they wanted to divorce their husbands, which was allowed anyway, they had to give reasons for the divorce in writing.

Being of Jewish background, the Apostle Paul's culture regarding marriage was different. For Paul, the first step on this important journey was the establishment of the marriage covenant, known as the betrothal. Jewish Marriage Customs tell us that:

The prospective bridegroom would travel from his father's house to the home of the prospective bride. There, he would negotiate with the father of the young woman to determine the price (mohar) that he must pay to purchase his bride. Once the bridegroom paid the purchase price, the marriage covenant was thereby established, and the young man and woman were regarded to be husband and wife. From that moment on the bride was declared to be consecrated or sanctified, set apart exclusively for her bridegroom. As a symbol of the covenant relationship that had been established, the groom and bride would drink from a cup of wine over which a betrothal benediction had been pronounced.[10]

Following the establishment of this marriage covenant, the groom would head back to his father's house where he would remain for the next twelve months. This length of time allowed the bride to make the necessary preparation for married life, while it allowed the man to get his living accommodations together in anticipation for the time he would bring home his bride to reside with him in his father's house.

[10] "Jewish Marriage Customs" http://www.biblestudymanuals.net/jewish_marriage_customs.htm (accessed March 16, 2015).

What Paul would have seen in Athens was clearly different from his culture. In a Jewish marriage there were no wedding gods and no sacrifices would be made as the Athenians did. For Paul and every Jewish believer, to have another God besides Yahweh, would be an abomination.

As is the custom of the Jews, when the twelve months (the period of separation) came to an end, the groom would go and get his bride to live with him. This usually happened at night time, a similar practice seen in Athens where the father of the bride gave her away to the groom as night time fell. Paul would have seen some other similarities as well where the wedding procession was concerned. The Athenians would have guests carrying torches just as in the Jewish culture. The groom along with his best man and other male escorts would lead what is referred to as a "torch like procession"

A closer look at Paul's culture revealed that when a Jewish bride was getting ready for marriage, she would await the arrival of her groom at a time not known by her. Even though she has that expectation of him coming, the exact time of his arrival would not be known. She would however be forewarned of the arrival of her groom by a shout that would precede his arrival. The Jewish groom would then receive his wife along with her female attendants, after which the entire wedding party would go to the groom's father's house to meet with those already assembled there. Jewish Marriage Customs states:

> Shortly after arrival the bride and groom would be escorted by the other members of the wedding party to the bridal chamber (huppah). Prior to entering the chamber, the bride remained veiled so that no one could see her face. While the groomsmen and bridesmaids would wait outside, the bride and groom would enter the bridal chamber alone. There in the privacy of that place they would enter into physical union for the first time, thereby consummating the marriage that had been covenanted earlier.[11]

One of the duties that the Athenians felt was necessary after marriage was that of having children. Therefore, at the birth of a child, the father would announce the birth by hanging an olive branch at the front door of the house. Ten days after the birth, the family would have a celebratory meal and give presents to the new baby.

Sadly, in this culture not all babies were wanted. After a baby was born, if the baby was unwanted, he or she would be left out in the open to die. This kind of treatment was not considered a crime in Athens. Some of these unwanted babies were however rescued by families who could not have children. If a mother was fortunate enough to afford a slave, then she could get some help to nurse the

---

[11] "Jewish Marriage Customs" http://www.biblestudymanuals.net/jewish_marriage_customs.htm (accessed March 16, 2015).

baby but if a mother was poor then she had to care for her own children.

As Paul walked the streets of Athens he would see the residents clad in tunics. This was their basic garment made from two rectangular pieces of cloth, which in most cases would be wool. Linen, a lighter cloth made from flax, was also used but in a limited way. As Paul visited the market place and synagogues, he could identify the poorer class of Athenians because they would be dressed in clothing made from a very coarse cloth which came from animal's hair. He could tell who the rich folks were because they were clad in brightly colored cloth.

The men were decked out in short tunics with a large piece of woolen cloth draped over it. This would be wrapped around the body. If the weather was cold, it could be pulled over the head to provide some warmth. The Apostle Paul would most likely be amazed at the boys he saw running around barefooted, but that was how they dressed during the summer months while the men wore shoes, light sandals or sturdy boots.

Athenian women wore a longer tunic that went all the way down to their ankles. As Paul moved about Athens he would see women dressed in simply tailored tunics much like those of the men but he would spot more elaborate ones that had sleeves and fasteners at the waist and the hips, from time to time. Even though the women's tunics were longer than the men's they were required to wear a large piece of woolen cloth draped over the tunic as well. For footwear, the women would be seen in light sandals.

Athenians took pride in how they looked. The men could wear their hair whatever length they wanted, long or short. The older men had beards but the young men opted for a clean shave. As hairdressing became popular, the upper classes were attended to by slaves or visited public barber shops. For the women, their pride was their hair. They wore it long, most times pulled back into a pony tail or as a bun while at other times they would also dress up their hair with ribbons and head scarves.

Married women wore their hair long with elaborately fashioned locks, advertising their marital status with their locks. Many Athenian women also dyed their hair red with henna and sprinkled it with gold powder, often adorning it with fresh flowers.

As we discover from the writings of Rosemary Rees, The Ancient Greeks' hairstyles and make-up took on a varied form also;

> Rich women folded their hair around headbands. Sometimes they bought wigs in the latest fashion. In Athens, men visited the beauty parlor as often as women did. They wanted to be fashionable, too.

[12] Rosemary Rees, *Understanding People In The Past; The Ancient Greeks* (Crystal Lake, IL: Heinemann Library, 1997), 13

Men and women both wore perfume. Women used chalk to whiten their faces and juice to redden their lips.[12]

On his daily walk in Athens, Paul, becoming acquainted with the culture could identify the slaves. They had short hair as they were not allowed to keep long hair. They were all owned by citizens of Athens. No Athenian could be a slave, so the slaves were always foreigners, those captured during war time. These slaves had no freedom whatsoever so they did all the work. Their owners did not have to work at all because they needed the time to attend assembly meetings and to participate in government affairs. The rich families had many slaves while the poorer families would have a few to help them.

Athenians did not like to work for a master. They preferred to work for themselves because it made them more independent so most of them worked as farmers, even though the farmlands around Athens were not very fertile with the weather being hot and dry. Knowing this, the farmers had to choose their crops carefully. Few of the farmers were able to grow cereals such as wheat used for bread. They also cultivated fruit and vegetables in the valleys because there was good soil there. Grapes and olive trees grew well in soils that were considered poor. Some of the crops that Paul would have seen were grapes, barley, various types of beans and olives that were pressed to make olive oil. Most families raised sheep and goats on the mountainside but raising cattle was difficult.

Athenians who lived in the city had other jobs. In the city of Athens, Paul would have seen various craftsmen who set up workshops to manufacture the items needed by the townspeople. Only men were craftsmen. The occupations included Carpenters who would make the wooden furniture needed. There were Smiths who made knives and armor from iron and bronze. There were potters who made the cups, bowls, jars and plates needed. They had folks who made baskets using reeds. These baskets were used to store fruit, grain and wool.

Athens was a lively place, a city buzzing with activities and an ever increasing population. It attracted people from all over the world. Traders came to Athens to get their silver, olive oil, pottery and wine so they could buy extra wheat grain. This city was famous for the skills of the people. A study of ancient Greece revealed:

> Athens was famous for the skill of its craftspeople. Painters, potters, metalworkers, carpenters and leather workers were among those who had workshops and factories in the city. Pottery was used for storage vessels of all kinds, and for other objects such as cookers, grills and baths. Athenian pottery was sold throughout the Mediterranean. Most potters had their workshops in an area called the Kerameikos (the English word 'ceramic', which means pottery, comes from this word).[13]

---

[13] Peter Connolly, *Ancient Greece* (Oxford University Press, 2001) 48

Athenians celebrated seventy public holidays every year. Most of them were religious festivals. Most of these celebrations showcased sports and other competitions, the biggest of which was the Panathenaic Games, held every four years. These games were only open to men. Married women were not even allowed to watch this event. There was the Running event, the Pentathlon which included five events; long jump, throwing the discus, sprint, wrestling and throwing the javelin. There was boxing, horse races, poetry, dancing and torch carrying relay race events as well.

In addition to sports and games, the Athenians loved music, poetry and theatre as well. Moving around the city, Paul most likely would have seen **the Odeon**, a large covered hall built for musical events. Boys and men played musical instruments in the Odeon.

Every large city in Greece had a theatre. The world's first known theatre performances took place on the slopes just north of the Acropolis in Athens. They started out as plays with only small scenes within the general celebrations but were so popular that they eventually became a drama competition lasting all day. The actors were all men who performed in huge open air theatres while people crowded in to watch. The best seats went to important citizens such as judges and priests. These plays which were centered on Greek gods and heroes, were sponsored by rich Athenians who paid for the actors, the sets and the costumes as well.

On a trip to Athens, Paul would be able to see one of three types of plays - tragedies, satires or comedies. **Tragedies** were about sad and solemn objects. **Satires** made fun of something serious while **comedies** made people laugh. The Athenians enjoyed comedies because they made fun of politicians and other important people. Some of these plays are still being performed in Greece today.

The Daily Market Place

While in transit in Athens, Paul went around the city and seeing the level of idolatry there, he sought to educate the Athenians and the foreigners about the true God, Yahweh. One of the places he held meetings to address the matter of polytheism was in the market place also known as the Agora.

The Agora or marketplace was a large open space in the center of most Greek cities. Originally the word **"agora"** meant a meeting or assembly but later came to mean a marketplace. Meetings of the ekklesia were initially held in the Agora but were later moved to the Pnyx, a hill near the Agora. Simply put, the Agora was an open area surrounded by shops and public buildings. At one time or the other it was used for public debating, for elections, for trials, for buying and selling as well as other kinds of businesses. The Agora was home to other government buildings and the law courts and the prison were also situated there.

The market place, or Agora was divided into areas of specialty. A walk into the market place would reveal an area that catered solely to "Cheese" or "Fish" or "Wine", etc. Produce were not mixed. They were categorized. It would look like a common farmers' market in our day. The vendors, or market traders, as they were called, had their goods out on stalls to sell. There was a slight difference from our day in that, in Athens' market place, there were bankers who would be sitting at counters on the Agora, ready to lend money to people who needed to borrow.

On both sides of the marketplace there would be workshops for bronze workers, potters and those who carved stones. Lots of people went back and forth in this busy market place so it provided the Apostle Paul the perfect opportunity to hold his meeting with the customers there. This was a prime location and Paul took advantage of the environment to present his God, Yahweh to those present there.

Temples, law courts and the building where the assembly met were situated on the other two sides of the Agora. These temples are not equivalent to what we call temples today. They were built for their many gods and goddesses and each temple contained a shrine with a statue of the god to whom they prayed in it. Peter Connelly

explains:

> A temple was not a place where people regularly
> worshipped. The building was built to house a statue
> or other image of the god: it was the god's 'house'.
> People would go to the temple to ask the god for his
> or her favor. Often they would leave a small
> offering of food. The size of the temple building
> was a measure of the importance of the god in that
> city or community. Sacrifices were not made inside
> the temple, but at an altar or shrine outside it.[14]

Paul saw the gifts that people left in front of the

shrine. They were very religious so no doubt he saw them

praying at the outdoor altar as well. Athenians believed in

many gods and had many different ideas about them as

well. In that culture, they believed there were gods who

looked and behaved like humans.

If the Athenians wanted a special favor, they would

kill an animal and offer it to one of the many gods they

worshiped. If they needed a good harvest, they would

---

[14] Peter Connolly, *Ancient Greece* (Oxford University Press, 2001) 32

make a sacrifice to the gods in that respect. If they thought the gods were angry, they would make offerings as well. They held different festivals which Paul may well have witnessed while he attended the market place.

> Throughout the year there were festivals to different gods. The festival began with a procession, with music and singing, in which an animal to be sacrificed was led through the streets. The procession ended at the altar, which was outside the god's temple. The priest killed the animal on the altar, and parts of it were burned as an offering to the gods. The rest of the meat was cooked as a feast for the people at the festival.[15]

Athenian men spent most of their free time away from their homes. They loved to exercise at the gymnasium or chat with friends in the market place so this was a good location for the Apostle Paul to have discussions in which he presented Yahweh to them. At night time, the men would often be invited to dinner at a friend's house, so this way, the news of Yahweh would get

---

[15] Peter Connolly, *Ancient Greece* (Oxford University Press, 2001) 32

around during dinner discussion. Only men were at this dinner, which would consist of a simple meal.

Athenian women were not allowed to do the shopping, so the only opportunity for them to go to the marketplace was to fetch water from the fountain in the Agora. This chore they carried out during the morning hours during which time they met, chatted and exchanged news. Slaves who were seeking to be hired would congregate at the edge of the Agora to be hired for work or to be bought by new owners.

Paul saw this location, the market place or the Agora, as the perfect place to hold conversations with the folks there. It seemed Paul was quite serious about teaching them about his God, Yahweh, because he did not just visit the marketplace once, but daily as the text says, "Therefore disputed he in the synagogue with the Jews, and with the devout persons, and in the market daily with them that met with him."[16]

In a city filled with great thinkers and very intelligent people, the Apostle Paul was on a mission to turn them from the service of idols to the service of the true and living God, Yahweh in Christ. His task was great because there were very few, if any, believers in Athens. Here, where human learning most flourished, idolatry most abounded.

---

[16] Acts 17:17 (King James Version)

4 PHILOSOPHICAL AND RELIGIOUS TEACHINGS

Philosophers

We read in the Old Testament that philosophers, also known as great thinkers, lived in Athens. The word **philosopher** means "*lover of wisdom*". It was some of these men who approached Paul in Athens, wanting to know what he was telling the people who gathered to listen to him. These philosophers were interested in all kinds of knowledge. Some studied mathematics while some were more interested in people's characters and their behavior.

Others had an interest in the natural world. In his writings, Aristotle and Scientific Thought, Steve Parker writes;

> The Greeks visited many lands and encountered different religions and customs. Some began to question their own beliefs and assumptions, and this gave rise to the study of philosophy.
> The term "philosophy" comes from an ancient word *philosophos*, which is Greek (of course) for "lover of wisdom."[1]

Philosophy, which actually began in Ancient Greece somewhere around 600 BC, is said to be a complex subject. It addressed questions such as where do our beliefs, knowledge and thoughts actually come from? How do we know what we know? How can one decide what is right from what is wrong, what is good or bad or even what is true or false? Philosophy also addresses the meaning of certain words such as reality, truth and knowledge.

---

[1] Steve Parker, Aristotle and Scientific Thought (Chelsea House Publishers, 1995), 7

The first Philosophers went on a journey to find general underlying principles that would explain the world in which they lived. According to Steve Parker, "They introduced methods of reasoning, logic, observation, and even some experiments. Into these surroundings came two of the greatest philosophers – Plato and his pupil Aristotle."[2]

Athens, like much of Greece was filled with philosophers during Paul's visit and even long before his visit, there were many philosophers there. Among these notable philosophers was Democritus who suggested that all matter was made of tiny units that were indivisible. These tiny units are now known as atoms. There was the Greek Mathematician, Pythagoras of Samos, who believed that mathematics could answer most questions and that all things are numbers. Another philosopher was Thales of

---

[2] Steve Parker, Aristotle and Scientific Thought (Chelsea House Publishers, 1995), 7

Miletus who suggested that all things came from water and consist of water in different forms. He was the first known scientific philosopher. Anaxagoras had a theory that every substance was a mixture containing a little of everything and a pure element could never be obtained.

Then there was Hippocrates of Cos, known as the Father of Medicine. It is believed that he began the era of scientific medicine. Steve Parker explains, "The ancient Greeks, most importantly Hippocrates and his colleagues, began the era of scientific medicine. Before their time, and in many places since, medicine was tied up with religion and superstition. The physician rarely even examined the patient. He guessed the illness from a religious "sign."[3] Hippocrates and his followers taught that the physician should examine and observe the patient and use the symptoms to work out the illness. The

---

[3] Steve Parker, Aristotle and Scientific Thought (Chelsea House Publishers, 1995), 9

physician was told to only give medicine when necessary and that they should check the patient at a later time to see what effects the medicine may have caused as well as to see what course the disease had taken. Hippocrates theory was that, a physician could only gather real knowledge and make progress in medicine by observing and keeping records.

Another philosopher of that time was Anaximander, who was said to be Thales' student. Anaximander is credited with being the author of the first scientific book on the history of the universe. The great thinker Anaximenes, believed that everything was made of different forms of air. He taught that rainbows had nothing to do with God but were instead natural.

The philosopher, Aristotle who lived over two thousand, three hundred years ago, was considered as foremost among the ancient Greek philosophers. "He thought and wrote about a huge range of subjects, and in particular his philosophy of science and from nature study to physics, was to shape scientific thought for centuries to come. Many of his ideas are long out of date. But, if a person had to be singled out, perhaps as the "Grandfather of Science" one of the favorites would be Aristotle." [4]

Socrates was another of the great philosophers who made an impact on the people during his time. He lived in Athens all his life and although it is said that he wrote nothing he had a quest for true knowledge and wisdom. It was his pupil Plato, who wrote about him. His philosophy was that if people asked themselves questions in the correct way, they could find the answers within themselves and in turn could teach themselves. Out of this came what is known as "dialogue", the Socratic tradition of furthering knowledge by asking questions. Socrates was later in life,

---

[4] Steve Parker, Aristotle and Scientific Thought (Chelsea House Publishers, 1995), 4

accused of corrupting young people in Athens by his questioning and so was sentenced to death by drinking poison.

In a grove on the outskirts of Athens, stood an academy, a school where people could think, develop understanding and acquire knowledge. It was founded by the philosopher, Plato. The author Steve Parker states:

> The Academy was not like the typical schools we have today. There were few set subjects and lessons. Little importance was put on practical studies such as engineering, physics, and chemistry. There were few attempts to carry out observations or experiments or to investigate the real world of objects and events.
> Instead, Plato encouraged his students to let their minds and thoughts roam free. They strove to break away from daily realities, from what happens in the physical world, and from the things we see, hear and feel around us.[5]

Plato spoke about things he called "Forms". These "Forms" explain our ideas about things such as justice,

---

[5] Steve Parker, Aristotle and Scientific Thought (Chelsea House Publishers, 1995), 13

goodness, beauty and so on. "Forms" also explains how we know the truth about such things. "From his work came the Platonic Tradition, in which matters of the mind and the ideas behind words were the true basis of existence."[6] The common aim of these philosophers was to find knowledge and understanding and this purpose, they followed so hard in the same way as if it were a religion.

Some philosophers taught and discussed while walking, pacing to and fro. They discussed anything from logic to philosophy, rhetoric to politics as well as ethics. Some of them had the ideology of pure thought in the mind while others dealt more with the real world and the object and events in it.

Those philosophers who used "logic" simply utilized the art and process of using language to reason from one fact or statement to another. They reasoned that facts do

---

[6] Steve Parker, Aristotle and Scientific Thought (Chelsea House Publishers, 1995), 13

not simply exist. They had to be expressed as well as understood in terms of words and language.

Epicureanism & Stoicism

Paul became known in Athens due to his meetings in the synagogue with the Jews and the devout persons and his daily market place meetings. Therefore, he drew the attention of the philosophers in that city. "Then certain philosophers of the Epicureans, and Stoicks, encountered him."[7]

Epicureans were those who belonged to the sect of Epicurius, the philosopher. The name Epicurean actually means "a helper: defender". Epicurius is said to have written over three hundred pieces of work, but only fragments of his writings remain today. He believed that we could all find a way to be happy, so he based his

---

[7] Acts 17:18 (King James Version)

philosophy on just that, accomplishing a happy and satisfied life without feeling fear and pain.

> It was by living in 'seclusion', not being involved in politics, a self sufficient life without pursuing wealth or glory. It was also emphasized the importance of a close circle of friends, that you could trust and participate in enjoying the lesser glorified objects in life, such as food and science. Believing pleasure and pain to be measures of what is good and bad. Epicurus (as opposed to Aristotle) believed death is the end of the body and the soul, so it should not be feared.[8]

It is said that Epicurus' teachings showed that unlike the common belief at the time, he believed gods were not concerned with humans and that they neither rewarded nor punished humans. Epicureanism taught that when a person is not suffering from pain, he is no longer in need of pleasure and has therefore entered a state of what is considered as perfect mental peace.

---

[8] 2003-2012 University Press Inc. "Epicurus"
www.ancientgreece.com/s/People/Epicurus (Accessed April 7, 2015).

Epicureanism is said to have consisted of a way of life directed at worldly happiness, so in essence, what Epicurus was doing was not just psychologically satisfying, but rather in accord with the true nature of things.

The Oxford Companion to Philosophy states that "Epicurus established his school of philosophy in 306 BC just outside the walls of Athens where he purchased a house for accommodation and a garden in which teaching took place." [9]

Epicureanism was not only found in Athens, Greece, but also in Tyre, Sidon, Alexandria, Gadara (in Syria) and elsewhere in the Hellenistic world. This school of thought was clearly not in sync with what the Apostle Paul was teaching here in Athens. The philosophers clearly didn't know of this God that Paul talked about, because they

---

[9] Ted Honderich, *The Oxford Companion to Philosophy* (Oxford New York: Oxford University Press), 239

claimed that he was presenting a strange god to them. Paul

openly declared the resurrection to the Athenians because

his personal experience with Jesus Christ solidified the fact

for him, that Jesus Christ rose from the dead. Paul

steadfastly believed and preached about the resurrection,

not just of Jesus Christ but also of the saints.

13 But I would not have you to be ignorant, brethren, concerning them which are asleep, that ye sorrow not, even as others which have no hope.

14 For if we believe that Jesus died and rose again, even so them also which sleep in Jesus will God bring with him.

15 For this we say unto you by the word of the Lord, that we which are alive and remain unto the coming of the Lord shall not prevent them which are asleep.

16 For the Lord himself shall descend from heaven with a shout, with the voice of the archangel, and with the trump of God: and the dead in Christ shall rise first:

17 Then we which are alive and remain shall be caught up together with them in the clouds, to

meet the Lord in the air: and so shall we ever be with the Lord.

18 Wherefore comfort one another with these words.[10]

Since Epicureans believed in happiness here on earth and no resurrection, they would no doubt be concerned and maybe angry at Paul's doctrine of life after death. They followed a man who himself did not believe in any gods except in name. They denied that they exercised any government over the world or its inhabitants. They believed in eating as you like and that pleasure was the only end in life.

There was nothing sacred about God in their religion. They do not believe in immortality of the soul and since they did not believe in the resurrection of the body either, Paul's message would have certainly disturbed them. They would not want to be accountable for the life they lived on

---

[10] 1 Thessalonians 4:13-18 (King James Version)

earth and certainly would not have wanted any hindrance to enjoying the pleasures of life. They would not want to affect the conscience in a negative way either so Paul's speech would definitely be a cause of concern for the Epicureans.

The second set of philosophers that encountered Paul were the Stoicks. These were those who followed the teachings of Zeno of Citium. He was a teacher at Athens and it is believed that he occupied a particular porch in Athens, hence the word "Stoics" for them meant, "of the portico."

The Stoicks, unlike the Epicureans, believed in gods but they did not believe in any supreme god. They believed that all human affairs were governed by fate and that no good came from various deities or gods. They believed that man should be free from passion and should be moved by neither joy nor grief, pleasure nor pain.

According to the Oxford Companion to philosophy, "Stoicism placed ethics in the context of an understanding of the world as a whole, with reason being paramount both in human behaviour and in the divinely ordered cosmos."[11]

It further explains:

> Stoic ethics indicated that if a perfectly wise, i.e. virtuous, man saw his child in danger of drowning (say), he would try to save it; but if he failed he would accept this without feeling distress or pity, and without his happiness being diminished. Since everything that happens is governed by divine providence his failure must have been for the best, even if he could not understand why. Moreover, moral virtue is the only good, and wickedness the only evil; so the child's death was not itself an evil. Furthermore, since moral virtue is the only good, and being perfectly virtuous the wise man will by definition have done the best he could, there is nothing for him to regret.[12]

---

[11] Ted Honderich, *The Oxford Companion to Philosophy* (Oxford New York: Oxford University Press), 852

[12] Ibid., 852-853

Judaism

Based on the recording in Acts, there was at least one Jewish synagogue in Athens. Paul visited this synagogue on a weekly basis and he used it possibly on the Sabbath Day to reason with the people while he used the market place on a daily basis to evangelize. In the Commentary of the New Testament, Robert H. Gundry explains it this way;

> By noting Paul's inner exasperation with Athenian idolatry, Luke appeals to prospective converts who have themselves become disaffected with idolatry and thus open to the gospel. "Therefore" means that the irritation motivated Paul to use both the local synagogue and the marketplace as venues for conversing with people for the purpose of getting them to believe in Jesus. So far as the synagogue is concerned, Paul was limited to Sabbath days. But the marketplace provided him a daily opportunity for evangelism, and he took advantage of it.[13]

---

[13] Robert H. Gundry, *Commentary On The New Testament* (Massachusetts: Hendrickson Publishers Marketing, LLC, 2010), 532-533

The Jews' religion, known as Judaism, is said to be one of the world's most long-lived religious traditions. According to Judaism: World Religions, "This respected ancient religion arose in the Near East some 3,500 years ago, in the mid-second millennium BCE (Before the Common Era), or 1500 BC among monotheistic religions, or those whose followers believe in only one true god. It is most probably the oldest."[14]

Even though the Jews were in a land filled with strange gods, they held firm to the tenets of their faith. Jews believe that there is only one universal God. This God, they believe is not only the God of the Jews but the God of all peoples and nations. His name is Yahweh, the one who created the entire universe. Being a part of this religion, the Apostle Paul believed that Yahweh was all-knowing, perfect, holy, eternal, and did not have any

---

[14] Martha A. Morrison and Stephen F. Brown, *JUDAISM WORLD RELIGIONS* (New York: Infobase Publishing, 2006), 6

physical form. The Jewish people knew Him to be in control of nature and history and is far greater than human beings can fathom. They worshipped God directly and were forbidden to worship any statue or image or any material likeness of God like those in the ancient Near East were doing.

Paul, being a Jew himself, believed that Jews were specially chosen by God to receive His Law. The covenants or agreements that were made by God and humankind are credited for this belief. The early Hebrews likewise believed in their covenant with Yahweh and like their patriarch Abraham, they believed in the divine promises made to them from ancient times.

Who or what is a Jew? Jews are found in many countries throughout the world. Are they the same as Hebrews, Israelites, or Israelis? Rebecca Weiner explains in her writings on "Judaism, Who Is A Jew";

The original name for the people we now call Jews was Hebrews. The word "Hebrew" (in Hebrew, "Ivri") is first used in the Torah to describe Abraham (Gen. 14:13). The word is apparently derived from the name Eber, one of Abraham's ancestors. Another tradition teaches that the word comes from the word "eyver," which means "the other side," referring to the fact that Abraham came from the other side of the Euphrates, or referring to the fact Abraham was separated from the other nations morally and spiritually. Another name used for the people is Children of Israel or Israelites, which refers to the fact that the people are descendants of Jacob, who was also called Israel.[15]

Like any Jew, Paul visited the synagogue while in transit in Athens. It was here that he did some of his reasoning with the Jews and God fearing Greeks. In their culture, Jews go to synagogues to meet the need for human contact, spiritual fulfillment and intellectual stimulation.

---

[15] Jewish Virtual Library "Judaism; Who Is A Jew" www.jewishvirtuallibrary.org (Accessed April 28, 2015).

A review of Jewish traditions, customs and values for today's families, brought to light the fact that the term "Synagogue" used in this account of Paul's visit is not a Hebrew word. Anita Diamant and Howard Cooper explains: "Actually, "synagogue" is not a Hebrew word. The term appeared in the Christian Bible as the Greek translation of the term *beit k'nesset*, meaning "house of assembly."[16]

Whether Synagogue or House of Assembly though, this was the weekly meeting place of the Jews in Athens, and Paul met them there to reason with them about the level of idolatry that surrounded their Jewish families.

---

[16] Anita Diamant and Howard Cooper, *Living A Jewish Life* (New York: Harper Collins Publishers, 1991) 118.

5 WORSHIP OF THE GODS AND GODDESSES

Worship was of great importance in ancient Greece. Looking at the daily life of the Ancient Greeks, Fiona Macdonald states, "Worship was very important in ancient Greece; it was part of everyday life. Men, women, and children said prayers, made offerings and took part in religious festivals. They visited temples, where gods and

---

[1] Fiona Macdonald, *Gods & Goddesses In The Daily Life Of The Ancient Greeks* (Columbus, OH: McGraw-Hill Children's Publishing, 2002), 10

goddesses lived. They also asked for divine help at key

moments such as births, weddings, and funerals."[1]

The gods that the Athenians worshiped ranged from

those living in forests and streams to those living in the

mountains.

> The Greeks worshiped many different kinds of gods
> and goddesses. Some were nature-spirits, living in
> mountains, forests, and streams. Others were local
> or tribal gods who watched over just one city or
> tribe. A few were "borrowed" from neighboring
> peoples. But the best known and most powerful
> group of gods and goddesses was the "family"
> headed by Zeus and his wife Hera. Known as the
> "Olympians," because they lived on Mount
> Olympus in northern Greece, legends told how they
> fought and conquered earlier, more primitive, gods –
> the Titans, children of Uranus (heaven) and Gaia
> (earth).[2]

Mount Olympus is the highest mountain in Greece and

is said to be the home to their twelve great gods and

goddesses also known as the Olympians. It was the

lightest and most worshipped mountain of Greece, a

---

[2] Ibid.

magnificent place with lots of forests and gorges and summits of different heights. This place boasts mild climate and is said to be surrounded by Uranus, which is considered by the Greeks, the heaven. According to history, it never rained on Mount Olympus nor was it ever windy. It is said that only some clouds were appearing from time to time to isolate the god's kingdom from the outside world and bless the world with water.

It was an important part of the Greek culture for its citizens to keep in close contact with their gods. The citizens of Athens believed these gods looked like human beings but they had powers unlike those of human beings, and were all around. Athenians felt that even though their gods and goddesses were invisible, their power was evident in natural forces such as the rumbling of thunder, the sounds of the wind and even the crashing of the waves on the shore. These gods were believed to have power to change themselves into creatures like eagles and bulls and they even married each other. They subscribed to the ideology that these gods lived forever by sipping nectar which was their life giving drink, and their special food, ambrosia.

Religion for them played a central part in their lives. They displayed their affection, respect and honor for their gods by holding festivals. Each Greek city, including Athens, organized its own festivals that would honor its favorite local gods. There would be no normal work on these days, as the citizens would engage in the chanting of hymns and taking part in processions and sacred rituals. Athenians also believed they could use sacrifices to bargain with the gods. Writing on the topic 'Gods All Around", Fiona Macdonald explains what sacrifices were used: "These included food and drink, incense, and valuable goods such as gold and silver and fine embroidered cloth. Many families offered small sacrifices at their own household altar every day. In return, they expected the gods to protect them from hunger, sickness, and other misfortune."[3]

THEIR GODS

ZEUS

The king of the Athenian gods was called Zeus, so no doubt Paul must have seen his temple all adorned. Zeus is said to be the Greek god who brought order to the world by defeating his father, Cronus and the whole race of Titans. Considered to be the most powerful god on Mount Olympus, the Athenians believed that Zeus ruled over heaven and earth from that location. It is believed that as the ruler of the skies, he makes the sun and moon to

[3] Fiona Macdonald, *Gods & Goddesses In The Daily Life Of The Ancient Greeks* (Columbus, OH: McGraw-Hill Children's Publishing, 2002), 40

operate and he even changes the seasons. The citizens of Athens believed that Zeus upheld justice and the law, so he would hurl thunderbolts at wrongdoers when he was angry. Another characteristic that the Athenians attributed to Zeus was that he was friendly and hospitable and fell in love often. According to the Athenians, Zeus was married to Hera who was believed to be very jealous. His Roman name is Jupiter.

POSEIDON

To the Athenians, the second most powerful of their gods was Poseidon. He was considered the god of the sea and like the sea, he was thought to be calm and gentle or at times, rough and dangerous. According to Fiona Macdonald's findings:

> The sea played an important part in many Greek peoples' lives. Most towns and villages were built close to the coast or on islands. Fish and shellfish,

caught fresh from the sea, provided the most important source of protein in most Greek families' meals. Travel by sea was also faster and easier than travel across the mountainous Greek mainland. The seas surrounding Greek lands were usually calm in the summertime, but could be rough and stormy in winter.[4]

This god, the Athenians believed could raise terrible storms or choose to calm them just by wielding his three pronged spear. In addition to his rulership of the sea, it is said that Poseidon was also the god of earthquakes and tidal waves, which he would cause to come against those who made him angry. It is believed that he dried up the lakes and rivers that were being used by the people whom he did not trust.

Athenians use the sea for trading so they would pray to Poseidon, asking for his protection on the waters. It is said

---

[4] Fiona Macdonald, *Gods & Goddesses In The Daily Life Of The Ancient Greeks* (Columbus, OH: McGraw-Hill Children's Publishing, 2002), 29

that whenever the waters became calm, it was as a result of Poseidon riding his golden chariot over the seas.

In addition to having an inscription in his honor in Athens, a sports festival called the Isthmian Games, was held in his honor, in the trading port of Corinth in southern Greece every two years. Poseidon, the Athenians god of the seas, is believed to have been married to Amphitrite but still fell in love with other women almost as often as their most powerful god, Zeus. The Romans knew this god as Neptune.

HADES

Among the many gods in Athens, was the god known as Hades which also bears the Roman name of Pluto. For Athenians, this is the god of the underworld: death and burial, also known as the Lower World. Hades was the king of the underworld, a place considered to be a cold and gloomy region where the souls of the dead lived. Athenians believed that the Lower World was filled with wailing ghosts, howling furies, shrieking bats and lost and evil souls. In their mythology, after entering the Lower World, that soul is not allowed to leave. Hades' wife, Persephone, who lived on earth before becoming his wife, was the only exception to this rule. The Athenians believed that a fierce three-headed dog called Cerberus, stood guard to the entrance of the Underworld. This animal would attack souls who tried to leave, but would not pose a threat to the newly arrived dead souls.

Loyalty for the gods was paramount in Athens. They believe Hades, even though stern and grim, was also merciful, just and fair. He was also worshipped as the god of wealth, as we discover in the writings of Leonard Everett Fisher: "Hades owned everything precious that lay in the ground – every piece of gold and silver every diamond, ruby, emerald and gem."[5]

Hades is believed to be Zeus' brother. However, unlike his brother Zeus, Hades rarely visited Mount Olympus or the land of the living, because he presided over the world of the dead.

ARES

Athenians had a god of war. His name was Ares, the god of war, furious rage and mindless violence. His Roman name was Mars, a fiery, bloody character. Leonard Fisher explains,

> Ares was a fiery, bloody character. Not even his parents liked him. He thrived on violence, battles and wars. The Earth growled and groaned beneath him as he moved. Even though he joined wars on Earth among humans, he was not as powerful as he appeared. There were times when he was driven

[5] Leonard Everett Fisher, *The Olympians Great Gods and Goddesses of Ancient Greece* (New York, NY: Holiday House, 1984), 12

from battlefields by humans who preferred living in peace to fighting one another.[6]

Ares, although thought to be handsome and very manly, was not admired. As a matter of fact, the symbols of the vulture and the dog were used to represent him. He was fierce and strong and had an uncontrollable temper. Athenians and Greeks at large did not appreciate his ways of war, because they wanted a civilized and orderly way of living. They wanted to spend their days peacefully and so dreaded the chaos and suffering that war brought to them.

Ares was Zeus' brother but unlike his brother Zeus, not many of his stories have survived. In spite of being a god, the people preferred not to think about him because his stories are not pleasant ones.

---

[6] Leonard Everett Fisher, *The Olympians Great Gods and Goddesses of Ancient Greece* (New York, NY: Holiday House, 1984), 26

APOLLO

The most loved of all the gods on Mount Olympus was the handsome, talented, honest and charming Apollo. He was worshipped as the god of light and truth; the god of healing; the god of archery; the god of music and the god of prophecy. His Roman name was still Apollo but he was often called Phoebus which means "shining." Apollo was worshiped in some cities as the god of the Sun. Athenians believed that he was Zeus' son, who along with his twin sister, Artemis, protected animals and possessed power to heal or harm.

Athenians adored this god for his skill in playing his golden lyre and singing songs, because they believed that music had magical power. Fiona Macdonald explains:

> The Greeks believed that music had magical power that could inspire love, soothe angry feelings, raise dull spirits, or even tame wild animals and move

heavy stones. They enjoyed singing, dancing, and listening to music at feasts, family parties, theater performances, and religious festivals. Music echoed the feelings of people taking part in wedding and funeral processions and encouraged Greek soldiers as they marched off to war.[7]

Apollo is also known for teaching Athenians how to comfort and cure those who were sick and ailing. To the Athenians, Apollo was full of goodwill wherever he went. His temple, as seen by Apostle Paul, may have displayed symbols of Crow, Dolphin, Laurel or Lyre.

HERMES

For Athenians, Hermes was the god who was the messenger of travel and trade. He was revered as the god of motion, the god of sleep and dreams, the god of commerce and the god of travelers.

---

[7] Fiona Macdonald, *Gods & Goddesses In The Daily Life Of The Ancient Greeks* (Columbus, OH: McGraw-Hill Children's Publishing, 2002), 25

He was said to be graceful, bright, clever and quick-witted. Describing his job, Leonard Fisher writes:

> He was Zeus's messenger. He wore a winged golden helmet–sometimes a silver one–to protect himself from bad weather. His golden winged sandles gave him speed. And he carried a magic golden wand or *caduceus*, a gift from Apollo, to guide him on his journeys. One of his jobs was to lead the dead to Hades' Lower World. Another was to watch over tradesman and travelers. He also helped travelers sleep well and have pleasant dreams. Hermes invented fire, written music, boxing and the lyre, his gift to Apollo.[8]

Athenians consider him to be the lookout god who would carry news between the gods on Mount Olympus and the humans. Due to the many journeys made by Hermes, he was worshiped as the god of travelers and merchants who traveled long distances. In addition to his regular job, it is said that he had another very special job. According to Fiona McDonald's discovery, "...he also had

---

[8] Leonard Everett Fisher, *The Olympians Great Gods and Goddesses of Ancient Greece* (New York, NY: Holiday House, 1984)

another, very special, duty – leading dead souls from Earth to the Underworld, their final home. He was given a special title when performing this task – Hermes Psychopompus"[9]

At his temple in Athens, symbols such as wands, winged sandals and winged helmets would be displayed for the folks to see. Hermes, also known by his Roman name, Mercury, was said to be the child of Zeus.

HEPHAESTUS

Of all the gods and goddesses on Mount Olympus, Athenians believed Hephaestus was the least good looking and that his mother hated him for his looks. He was said to be another of Zeus' children and was born with a deformed foot. He was said to be the only god born with a handicap.

[9] Fiona Macdonald, *Gods & Goddesses In The Daily Life Of The Ancient Greeks* (Columbus, OH: McGraw-Hill Children's Publishing, 2002)

In busy cities like Athens, Hephaestus was worship as the god of fire and metalworking. Athenians believed he turned rock into deadly bronze weapons and sometimes into beautiful gold jewelry. He was known as god of the forge, with his forge being under any erupting volcano. Athenians believed he was unhappily married to Aphrodite, the wife he worshiped but she betrayed him by having a string of love affairs. His Roman name was Vulcan and his symbols were Fire and Blacksmith's hammer.

DIONYSUS

Among the gods and goddesses of Athens, there was also a god of wine, drunkenness, dancing and theatre. He was said to be the son of Zeus. It is mostly the Athenian women that worshipped Dionysus. This included out of control behaviors with the women drinking and dancing.

ASCLEPIUS

The Athenians god of healing had a name. He was known as Asclepius and he controlled health and medicine. The people believed he was Apollo's son, born to a human mother. Famous for his skill at healing the sick, Athenians believed that this power was a gift by the gods. It is believed that Asclepius lived on earth as a human but became a god after his death. Legend has it that he was killed by Zeus who became angry with him and killed him with a thunderbolt.

Asclepius was not only worshiped in Athens as we find out. "Asclepius was worshipped at many places, but his most important sanctuary was at Epidaurus in southern Greece... People traveled long distances to sleep in the temple there, hoping that Asclepius would appear to them in a dream and cure them. Asclepius's sacred symbol was the snake. Therefore, many snakes lived in his temple as honored guests."[10]

When Athenians became ill they would take a trip to the temple of their god of healing, Asclepius. Priests were at this temple trying to cure those who were sick, by using a mixture of bathing, fasting, simple food, rests, herbs and magic. Those who were cured would have their names and details of their cure, carved on stone blocks in the temple for others to see.

In Greece, Asclepius was depicted as a kind, bearded man holding a serpent-entwined staff. Even though he is not seen in ancient Greek vase painting, statues of him are very common.

---

[10] Fiona Macdonald, *Gods & Goddesses In The Daily Life Of The Ancient Greeks* (Columbus, OH: McGraw-Hill Children's Publishing, 2002), 34

Their Goddesses

HERA

The queen of the gods was called Hera by the Athenians, but known to the Romans as Juno. She was said to be the beautiful sister of Zeus who took her to be his wife. Athenians considered Hera as the goddess of marriage and motherhood. Her life on Mount Olympus was said to be a difficult one as according to Leonard Fisher, "she spent much of her time in jealous rages, plotting either to destroy Zeus or to punish his lady friends."[11]

There is no doubt that among the gods worshiped in Athens, Paul would have seen Athenian women visiting Hera because she was revered as the god of the Greek women's lives. She was adored by married women and

---

[11] Leonard Everett Fisher, *The Olympians Great Gods and Goddesses of Ancient Greece* (New York, NY: Holiday House, 1984)

worshipped by women as the protector of marriage. Her husband, Zeus consulted her for help in ruling the other Olympians, but in her own life, Hera could not manage her husband. It is said that she was often left alone and feeling miserable, so she would display her anger by nagging her husband and terrorizing the women he loved. The Peacock and the Cow are the symbols associated with this goddess.

HESTIA

Athenians were big on family life. Their homes reflected traditional belief and values. An altar for prayers was built in each house. They also had a hearth where a fire was kept burning constantly. To them, there was a goddess who protected the home and family. She was called Hestia, goddess of the hearth: House and Home. Although she was not married, Athenians believed she watched over the homes and the hearth and was said to be the sweetest, gentlest and most generous of all the Olympians. Every human in Athens prayed to Hestia, and when a baby was born, it was carried around the hearth to symbolize its acceptance into the family that gathered by the hearth.

Hestia was so revered that Greek cities publicly honored her. According to writings on the Gods & Goddesses in The Daily Life Of The Ancient Greeks, "Greek cities kept a fire burning to honor Hestia in important government buildings. Officials made sacrifices there on behalf of all the citizens, and fire from the holy flame was given to warriors setting out on campaigns."[12]

Hestia's Roman name is Vesta and according to Greek history, two gods, Poseidon and Apollo wanted to marry her but she refused them, vowing to remain a virgin forever. It is said that she asked Zeus to protect her. He

[12] Fiona Macdonald, *Gods & Goddesses In The Daily Life Of The Ancient Greeks* (Columbus, OH: McGraw-Hill Children's Publishing, 2002), 10

agreed and gave her special blessings in return. The Athenians worshipped Hestia in every household, honoring her at all feasts, at the command of Zeus. Greek citizens moving from an old city to a newly built city, were required to carry live coals to the new city, in Hestia's name. Thus, her symbol is fire.

ATHENA

The protector of Athens was the goddess Athena. She was their goddess of wisdom, cleverness, and crafts as well as a goddess of war. There is a temple in Athens called the Parthenon. The city of Athens paid the entire cost of building the Parthenon, in honor of Athena. It houses her magnificent statue. Athena, who is also known as Minerva to the Romans, was said to have been born fully grown from the head of her father, Zeus, dressed in armor, after Zeus had swallowed Athena's pregnant mother, Metis.

The Apostle Paul, at the inscription to Athena would probably have seen in her tribute, that she hated war and would only have engaged in war to defend the side of right. He would have understood that to the Athenians, she was revered because she never lost a battle. Athenians gave Athena credit for creating the olive tree, inventing the ship, trumpet, plow and bridle. It is believed that Athena knew the secrets of mathematics and taught women everywhere to sew, spin, weave and cook. For the men, it is said she taught them the skill of carpentry, shipbuilding and pottery making.

Athena, the favorite child of Zeus, is credited for the invention of the double flute known as the **aulos**. The symbols of the Owl, Shield and Olive Branch are used to represent her.

APHRODITE

Athenians believed in love and beauty, so they had a goddess representing those areas of their lives. She was described as the beautiful, thoughtless, unfaithful and dangerous Aphrodite, goddess of love and beauty, who betrayed her husband and was not a good mother. These people in the city of Athens, along with fellow citizens of Greece took pride in looking good. They admired strong, healthy bodies in both women and men. Even though their clothing was simple, it was elegant.

Those who worshipped Aphrodite could not even agree as to whether she had parents or not. Some said she was the daughter of Zeus and Dione, while some insisted she had no mother nor father at all. Legend has it that she came from the foamy sea, later appearing on Mount Olympus. She was one who took pleasure in meddling with the hearts and minds of everyone else. She was jealous of anyone who looked beautiful, so she invented awful punishments for women who boasted about their good looks. Her Roman name was Venus and her symbols were the Dove, Sparrow, Swan and Myrtle.

ARTEMIS

The Greek goddess known as Artemis was more popularly known by her Roman name Diana. Said to be another child of Zeus and the twin sister of Apollo, Artemis is worshiped as the goddess of hunting, the goddess of the moon and the goddess of children.

Greek history said she was a skillful archer, shooting arrows that brought death to people throughout Greece. Athenians believed that even though she would chase stags and other wild animals with a silver bow and arrow, she would protect the young animals and take care of young children, in her position as goddess of the hunt.

It is also said that she had the power of healing and would fiercely defend her worshippers.

Artemis also known as Diana, was connected to the moon as a symbol of purity. She was never married and was believed to be a virgin. Fiona Macdonald states:

> Mothers in childbirth prayed to Artemis for help and protection. Brides also made offerings to her on the eves of their weddings. This was because, as a virgin, Artemis had never known the pain of giving birth. Looking after babies and children was one of Greek women's most important tasks. Wealthy women hired wet nurses...and slaves to help feed their babies, and to make sure they were kept clean, warm and comfortable.[13]

It is said that Artemis could curse cities and bring deadly diseases to them. Her symbols are the Stag, Moon and Cypress.

DEMETER

---

[13] Fiona Macdonald, *Gods & Goddesses In The Daily Life Of The Ancient Greeks* (Columbus, OH: McGraw-Hill Children's Publishing, 2002), 22

The goddess Demeter was the goddess of all growing things; corn, food and farming. Athenian farmers produced grain crops, so they believed that Demeter gave the gift of grain to humans, along with the first ever fig tree.

Since Demeter did not have a temple on the high wide open places, it is very unlikely that the Apostle Paul would have seen anything in her honor, among the many temples and shrines he came in contact with in Athens. Demeter was instead worshiped in ceremonies hidden underground. Athenians honored her at a special festival attended only by women, once every year. The festival was called *Thesmophoria*.

6 PAUL'S SERMON: "THE UNKNOWN GOD"

The Inscription

Not much has been said about religious teachings in Athens. The Jews had synagogues there, but the name of their God was never mentioned among the many gods that were honored and worshipped throughout this city. It is almost unimaginable that a religious group such as the Jews would not have made the name of their God known.

In his quest to declare the one, true and living God, YHWH, to the Athenians, the Apostle Paul attracted the learned men to him. They in turn took hold of him, taking him to the city council that met on Mars' Hill. This council was called the Areopagus. These men demanded to know what Paul's "new" teaching was about. Seemingly, they had never heard about YHWH, even though Jews lived in that city and had their synagogue there.

These Athenian men claimed that the Apostle Paul was openly talking about some foreign gods of which they never heard, and so they demanded to know who these deities were. Let it be understood that Athenians and foreigners within Athens, were known for spending their time telling or hearing something new, so this *"new"* ideology fascinated them.

The Greeks feared they would offend a god by not giving him or her attention, so to avoid making such a mistake they used the label 'unknown god'. The fact that the name of the God worshiped by the Jews in Athens was not mentioned, nor did He have an altar bearing his name, can very well be that the Jews did not openly profess YHWH in Athens. Like today, so many Christians do not profess Jesus Christ in the work place, nor do they profess Him openly. During worship services at church, it is easy to profess Jesus Christ as Lord and Savior, so for many Christians it is relegated to just that.

Apparently, the Athenians were never told about Yahweh, the true God, so when Paul came into town talking about YHWH, they classified him as a **babbler**. The Greek terminology is *spermologo*s which literally means **"picking up seed" as a crow would do**. In essence, figuratively, they were saying that Paul was someone who picked up scraps of knowledge from here and there and passed them off as his own. According to the Strong-Lite concordance, metaphorically speaking, "babbler" meant lounging about the market place and picking up a substance by whatever may chance to fall from the loads of merchandise. In Athens, a babbler was also viewed as a parasite, one who is beggarly, abject and vile.

The Athenians said Paul seemed to be a proclaimer of foreign gods or deities. They branded him that way, because he proclaimed Jesus and the resurrection, as good news. Due to their limited knowledge of Judaism or even Christianity, they probably believed that Paul was proclaiming **"Jesus"** and **"resurrection"** as two different gods (deities) that were unfamiliar to them. It could be that the Athenians thought that **"Jesus"** and **"resurrection"** were a couple, as in male and female, because the Greek word for resurrection is *anastasis*, from which comes the feminine name, Anastasia, so they wanted an explanation immediately.

On the heels of this invitation to speak in what was considered as the most sacred and reputable court in the Gentile world, Paul quickly moved to educate the gathering using this perhaps, once in a lifetime opportunity. He opened up by commending them on their religiosity by saying **"Men of Athens, I see that you are very religious in all respects."** [1] The KJV renders it *"Ye men of Athens, I perceive that in all things ye are too superstitious."* The Greek terminology used here in the King James version of the Bible for "superstitious" is *deisidaimonesteros* (dice-ee-dahee-mon-es'-ter-os) meaning (in a good sense), reverencing god or the gods,

---

[1] *NET Bible* Acts 17:22

pious and religious. In this case, the term here meant that the people of Athens were more religious than others.

How did Paul figure they were so religious? He explained that as he was walking around, he noticed the devotions they had to their deities. Paul had seen the multiple temples, altars, statues and idolatrous images that were religiously honored by the Athenians and he was making it known that they did not go unnoticed. He saw it all. He however hastened to make mention of an inscription that caught his attention – the inscription which read **"TO THE UNKNOWN GOD"**

Ignorant Worship

Paul called the Athenians' worship of this God, ignorant worship. In essence Paul was telling them that they did not know this God, neither did they understand this God. The use of the term **"ignorant"** meant that they lacked information or intelligence concerning this unknown God.

The Athenians knew all their gods. According to their history, they knew the birth places of these gods, as well as the names of their spouses. They also could tell you the names of the gods' offspring. They knew what these gods liked and disliked and where they lived. These gods were so predictable that the Athenians could tell exactly what they would do when they were angry and when they were happy.

Each god had its own temple. These temples were beautifully decorated and were visited daily by the people around them. Athenians were required to visit these temples and shrines to perform rituals and sacrifices, through which the gods received their due. Sick folks would visit certain temples or shrines in an effort to receive healing.

The Athenians knew there was another God in addition to the many they revered, but the name of this God they did not know. They did not know anything about His ways, His likes or dislikes. They knew absolutely nothing about Him, only that He existed. To the Athenians, He was unknown. Unknown in the sense that they only knew of Him but didn't know Him in a personal way, not like they knew the other gods. They couldn't make a replica or representation of Him as they did of their many gods, simply because He was "unknown" to them. The Apostle Paul, understanding the people's level of intelligence regarding this unknown God, grabbed hold of the opportunity to declare God, YHWH to them.

The Nelson's NKJV Study Bible commentary states:

Because the men of Athens had scant knowledge of the Hebrew Scriptures, Paul started with the general revelation visible in creation itself. In the sixth century B.C. it was said that a poet from Crete name Epimenides turned aside a horrible plague from the people of Athens by appealing to a god of whom the people had never heard. An altar was built to honor this god, whom the Athenians now called the **UNKNOWN GOD**. Paul obviously knew of Epimenides; he quoted the poet in Titus 1:12.[2]

Paul's Declaration of YHWH

Paul started out his declaration of Yahweh by telling the Athenians that this "unknown god" they were worshiping, was in fact the same God that made the world they occupied, as well as everything in it. Seeing how they revered, respected and worshiped their many gods, Paul cautioned them that this God was different from those they knew, because unlike the other gods, this God did not

---

[2] *Nelson's NKJV Study Bible*, (USA: Thomas Nelson Publishers 1982) 1853

reside in temples made by humans. In essence, he was letting them know it would not be a good idea to build a temple for Yahweh, as they did for the other gods. "The God who made the world and everything in it is the Lord of heaven and earth and does not live in temples built by human hands."[3] In this discourse, Paul was showing the Athenians that man was made to worship God and not idols, pointing out to them that, idol gods shut up in the magnificent temples they were in, could not be the Unknown God, for they were less than the places in which they were contained. To talk this way, was a sure attack against all of Greek history, but Paul was all about declaring the truth here.

Paul remembered that prior to being a Christian, while he was witnessing the death of Stephen, Stephen declared boldly in Acts 7:48, that the most High did not

---

[3] Acts 17:24 KJV

dwell in temples made with hands, adding that Heaven is God's throne and Earth is his footstool. Even though Paul was not yet converted, those words took root in Paul's mental faculty and at the appointed time, those same words were recounted to a city full of idolaters.

The Apostle Paul was telling the Athenians that he in fact knew this Unknown God they were talking about and since he knew this God, he was going to tell them a thing or two about Him.

Even though not recorded in the Holy Scriptures, I visualize the Apostle Paul declaring to the scholars, in a very passionate delivery, that this God, is not, and cannot be worshiped with men's hands. The following description of Yahweh was coined by my Bishop and brother-in-law, Leroy Hawthorne and could have been used by Paul, had it been available then.

YHWH, is the eternal, independent and self-existent Being: He is the Being whose purposes and actions spring from within, without foreign motive or influence:

He is absolute in dominion; He is the most pure, the most spiritual of all essences;

He is infinitely benevolent, infinitely beneficent, infinitely true, and infinitely holy;

He is the cause of all being, the upholder of all things;

He is immeasurably happy, exceedingly perfect, without any finite or measurable limits; and eternally self-sufficient, needing nothing that He has made:

He is illimitable in His immensity, inconceivable in His mode of existence, and indescribable in His essence;

He is known fully only to HIMSELF, because an infinite mind can be fully apprehended only by itself.

He is the Being who, from HIS infinite wisdom, cannot slip up, make mistake or be deceived; and who, from His infinite goodness, can do nothing but what is eternally just, right and kind.[4]

Unlike the gods of Athens, Yahweh should not be viewed as a god that was in need of anything, because all life exists because of Him. This would be very difficult

---

[4] Hawthorne, Leroy. "God's Divine Calendar – Yahweh Elohim" (Bible Studies, Bible Truth Church of God International, Bronx, NY 2009

for the Athenians to comprehend, because all the other gods were catered to at one time or another by man. They were now learning that Yahweh was the God that gave breath, life and everything that was needed to live.

Surrounded by people who worshipped everything else but Yahweh, the Apostle Paul made it known to them, the power and might of Yahweh Elohim (God, the Creator) by letting these idol worshippers know that from one man, Yahweh made all the nations, that they should inhabit the whole earth. The explanation from Barnes' Notes on the Bible, on this verse, says:

> And hath made of one blood - All the families of mankind are descended from one origin or stock. However different their complexion, features, or language, yet they are derived from a common parent. The word blood is often used to denote "race, stock, kindred." This passage affirms that all the human family are descended from the same ancestor; and that, consequently, all the variety of complexion, etc., is to be traced to some other cause

than that they were originally different races created. See Genesis 1; compare Malachi 2:10. The design of the apostle in this affirmation was probably to convince the Greeks that he regarded them all as brethren; that, although he was a Jew, yet he was not enslaved to any narrow notions or prejudices in reference to other people. It follows from the truth here stated that no one nation, and no individual, can claim any pre-eminence over others in virtue of birth or blood. All are in this respect equal; and the whole human family, however they may differ in complexion, customs, and laws, are to be regarded and treated as brethren. It follows, also, that no one part of the race has a right to enslave or oppress any other part, on account of difference of complexion.[5]

Paul declared to the Athenians, that everyone on the earth was created to occupy the earth, so no one, nor any race, was in fact inferior or superior to the other. "This was the original command Genesis 1:28; and God, by his providence, has so ordered it that the descendants of one family have found their way to all lands, and have become adapted to the climate where he has placed them."[6]

---

[5] Bible Hub, http://biblehub.com/commentaries/acts/17-26.htm (Accessed July 3, 2015).

[6] Ibid.

A closer look at the terminology used in this portion of the discourse, provides a rich and rewarding understanding of the thoughts and ideology in that section of the world, at the time of Paul's unscheduled visit. As the people gathered to hear one considered by the elite, a babbler, they were now beginning to understand that not only were they of one blood, but they were now hearing that Yahweh's design for mankind on a whole, is to have them live all over the earth. This however came with the fixing of the seasons of the year, as well as the national boundaries within which they would live. Delving into the scriptures and its commentaries, the following was brought to light as recorded in Barnes' Notes on the Bible:

> And hath determined - Greek: ὁρίσας horisas. Having fixed, or marked out a boundary... The word is usually applied to a field. It means here that God "marked out," or "designated in his purpose," their future abodes.
> The times before appointed - This evidently refers to the dispersion and migration of nations. And it

means that God had, in his plan, fixed the times when each country should be settled, and the rise, the prosperity, and the fall of each nation. The different continents and islands have not, therefore, been settled by chance, but by a wise rule, and in accordance with God's arrangement and design.
And the bounds of their habitation - Their limits and boundaries as a people. By customs, laws, inclinations, and habits he has fixed the boundaries of their habitations, and disposed them to dwell there.[7]

Since this God being presented to the Athenians by Paul was the true and living God, Paul wanted them to understand that Yahweh wanted them to discover Him, to know His name and His character. Yahweh wanted them to understand that He was ever present and was never far away. They didn't have to go to Mount Olympus or to the shrines and temples to find Him, because He was present in their movement, present in every breath they took and present in every aspect of their lives.

[7] Bible Hub, http://biblehub.com/commentaries/acts/17-26.htm (Accessed July 3, 2015).

The Poet: Aratus

During the discourse, Paul quoted some of the Greek poets, who in times past, had given some form of acknowledgement, unknowingly to this "unknown" god. The quote, **"For we are also his offspring"** is said to be from the famous opening invocation to the Greek god, Zeus, written by the poet Aratus.

> [1] From Zeus let us begin; him do we mortals never leave unnamed; full of Zeus are all the streets and all the market-places of men; full is the sea and the havens thereof; always we all have need of Zeus. For we are also his offspring; and he in his kindness unto men giveth favourable signs and wakeneth the people to work, reminding them of livelihood. He tells what time the soil is best for the labour of the ox and for the mattock, and what time the seasons are favourable both for the planting of trees and for casting all manner of seeds. For himself it was who set the signs in heaven, and marked out the

constellations, and for the year devised what stars chiefly should give to men right signs of the seasons, to the end that all things might grow unfailingly. Wherefore him do men ever worship first and last. Hail, O Father, mighty marvel, mighty blessing unto men. Hail to thee and to the Elder Race! Hail, ye Muses, right kindly, every one! But for me, too, in answer to my prayer direct all my lay, even as is meet, to tell the stars.[8]

Aratus was a Greek Poet of Soli in Cilicia. It is said that he flourished c.315 to c.245 BC in Macedonia, Greece, and is best remembered for his poem on astronomy titled **"Phaenomena",** a book describing the constellations and weather signs. Aratus was certainly no stranger to the Athenians. Therefore, such a quote would have certainly caught the attention of those gathered in Paul's company. Paul was not endorsing Aratus' belief nor the Stoics' belief that the Greek god Zeus was the all-powerful god who created man. As a matter of fact, the

---

[8] "Phaenomena, Translated by G.R. Mair",
http://www.theoi.com/Text/AratusPhaenomena.html (Accessed February 2, 2015).

Apostle was letting them know that, yes, there is an all-powerful one who created us, so we are indeed His offspring, but this one who created us could not be Zeus, because this Divine Nature is not like gold or silver or stone. Paul advised them that the God he was presenting to them was not something shaped by art and man's devising, neither was He like those gods he saw them worshiping or paying respect to, as he scouted the city.

Recognizing that the Athenians worshiped their many gods out of ignorance, Paul admonished them that the true and living God, Yahweh, overlooked those times of ignorance, but now that knowledge was revealed to them, repentance was now necessary on their part, because a day of judgment was coming.

7 DOCTRINAL POINTS

Resurrection of The Dead

At the height of the well-known discourse by the Apostle Paul, we find him divulging to the Athenians that everyone will be judged in righteousness, by that special someone appointed by Yahweh to do so in the future. Those in attendance at the Areopagus possibly had puzzled looks on their faces, as well as questions on their minds regarding this future event.

Paul spoke with much confidence about this period of time; a sure event which he said would take place because Yahweh had demonstrated this in the resurrection of the dead. Without mentioning a name, the writings are clear that this judge is Jesus, the one whom Yahweh had raised from the dead.

At the very mention of the resurrection of the dead, the people were stirred. Paul found himself being mocked by some of the Athenians in the crowd, while there were others who pushed it aside with a promise of attending to the subject later.

In the crowd were Epicurean and Stoic philosophers and these people followed teachings not conducive to that of the Apostle Paul's. The Epicureans who followed the teachings of Epicurus, strongly believed that the chief end of humankind was pleasure and happiness. They were taught to rid themselves of the irrational fear of death.

Epicurus' argument was that death was nothing to man and it involved neither pleasure nor pain. Epicureanism also taught that the only thing bad for mankind is pain. For the Epicureans in the company of Paul, life was all about pleasure, they were never thinking about death, much more a resurrection. "This pleasure they believed, was attained by avoiding excess and the fear of death, by seeking tranquility and freedom from pain, and by loving other people. They believed that if gods existed they were not involved in the events on this earth."[1]

The Stoics on the other hand were no doubt aroused by this new doctrine surrounding the resurrection of the dead. They, being followers of Zeno, did not believe in the resurrection of the body either. They instead believed that "truly wise people would dominate their emotions, so that emotion would never influence them positively or

[1] *Nelson's NKJV Study Bible*, (USA: Thomas Nelson Publishers 1982) 1853

negatively. They accomplished this by believing that whatever happened was fate and therefore their lot in life. They taught a very frugal life, rejecting all luxury in food and clothing. Their philosophy was the opposite of the Epicureans".[2]

What was Paul alluding to when he spoke of the Judge on this "appointed day"? He wanted them to know that even though they did not believe in life after death, the resurrection of the body is real. Jesus Christ, Yahweh's Son, had already been crucified, buried and risen from the dead, as Paul knew it, so he was declaring to the Athenians that this Unknown God, Yahweh, had already raised the person appointed to be the Judge, from the dead. Even though Paul did not use the name Jesus Christ, we know our judge will be Jesus Christ as mentioned in the Holy

---

[2] Andrew Wommack Ministries, Teaching God's unconditional Love & Grace, Acts 17:18 http://www.awmi.net/bible/act_17_18 (Date accessed July 4, 2015)

Scriptures "For the Father judgeth no man, but hath committed all judgment unto the Son:"[3]

As a Jew, Paul would have believed in the resurrection of the dead. Even before Christianity came on the scene, it was recorded in Jewish Scriptures, known as the **Tanakh**, as we see in the book of Daniel "And many of them that sleep in the dust of the earth shall awake, some to everlasting life, and some to shame and everlasting contempt."[4]

As one who had a personal encounter with Jesus Christ, Paul, now being one of his followers, would have spoken about the resurrection with much conviction because he was now serving one who had been dead in times past and was now alive.

---

[3] John 5:22 KJV

[4] Daniel 12:2 KJV

According to scholars, it was while Paul was here in Athens that he wrote the book known as First Thessalonians. Paul wrote to the brethren in Thessalonica to encourage and reassure them. It was in this first letter that he spoke of the resurrection. No doubt he was reiterating what he already knew, so that the brethren would not lose hope. Having been confronted by folks from other religious orders who did not believe in the resurrection, Paul reminded the Thessalonian brethren of what will happen in the time to come, adding that they should comfort each other in the process as well.

> But I would not have you to be ignorant, brethren, concerning them which are asleep, that ye sorrow not, even as others which have no hope. For if we believe that Jesus died and rose again, even so them also which sleep in Jesus will God bring with him. For this we say unto you by the word of the Lord, that we which are alive and remain unto the coming of the Lord shall not prevent them which are asleep. For the Lord himself shall descend from heaven with a shout, with the voice of the archangel, and with the trump of God: and the dead in Christ shall

rise first: Then we which are alive and remain shall be caught up together with them in the clouds, to meet the Lord in the air: and so shall we ever be with the Lord. Wherefore comfort one another with these words.[5]

Paul was an ardent believer in the resurrection and he wasn't going to back down even in the face of been mocked and jeered. We see his firm belief made known, not just to the brethren at Thessalonica but as stated in one of his letters to the brethren at Corinth, Christ rose on the third day according to the Scriptures.

For I delivered unto you first of all that which I also received, how that Christ died for our sins according to the scriptures; And that he was buried, and that he rose again the third day according to the scriptures: And that he was seen of Cephas, then of the twelve: After that, he was seen of above five hundred brethren at once; of whom the greater part remain unto this present, but some are fallen asleep. After that, he was seen of James; then of all the apostles. And last of all he was seen of me also, as of one born out of due time.[6]

---

[5] 1 Thessalonians 4:13-18

[6] I Corinthians 15:3-8 KJV

Paul stated in the letter to the Corinthians that after Christ was risen from the dead he was seen by different people and he, Paul, saw Christ as well. Maybe, just maybe that's the reason why he walked away from the Athenians when they started to mock him about the doctrine of the resurrection, because Paul knew what he saw and it was no mistake that he had a personal encounter with the Christ that was once dead but is now alive and will come back one day to judge the world.

Visible Results Of The Sermon

The night at the Areopagus quickly came to an end, following the mention of the resurrection of the dead, by the Apostle Paul. The Stoics and the Epicureans had heard a mouthful from Paul and now they watched him leave Mars Hill.

Paul's discourse had been given and the Unknown God was now made known. The Athenians now had knowledge of this God, YHWH and also knew they had a responsibility to serve Him as the only true and living God. The choice was theirs. Paul had done his part and departed but he didn't leave Athens alone.

The message Paul gave on Mars Hill took a hold on some of the lives of the Athenians. As they listened keenly to the Apostle Paul, they believed the message he brought to them about the only true God, YHWH and His Son, Jesus Christ who is coming back to judge them. They seemingly wanted to hear more and learn more, so in the words of the King James Version, they "clave" unto Paul. The word **"clave"** is rendered in the Greek text, *kollaō* (kol-lah'-o) and means; 1) to glue, to glue together, cement, fasten together; 2) to join or fasten firmly together; 3) to join one's self to, cleave to.

Among these certain men who believed Paul's message was a member of the court of Areopagus. This Areopagite's name was Dionysius. After listening to that powerful discourse about Yahweh, this Athenian, Dionysius was converted to Christianity by Paul. It pays to know who your God is. Paul didn't just know of God, he knew God and so he was able to present Him that he knew, to those who didn't know Him.

From the beginning of time, women were always instrumental in God's work and as we see, Athens was no different. Paul's sermon had reached the heart of a woman named Damaris. Not much is said about her, only that she believed just like Dionysius and attached herself to Paul.

Although the numbers may not seem much, through his sermon that day at the Areopagus, Paul had won people for Christ. Along with Dionysius and Damaris, there were others who believed and followed Paul as well.

What if Paul had done what the Athenians do just because he was in Athens? What if we as Christians continue to do what the Romans do while we are in Rome? Can we win souls for the kingdom of God? Paul did not care about fitting in. His mission was to make the one Unknown God, known to all who would listen. Amidst the mocking and jeering, not caring that the Jews did not even support him, he stood up and boldly declared to the court and its attendees, that Yahweh is the name of this God they worshipped without knowing. By doing so……..

THE UNKNOWN GOD WAS NOW MADE KNOWN!

……..MISSION ACCOMPLISHED!

The Unknown God

Elohim spoke to Moses, "I am Yahweh. I appeared to Abraham, Isaac, and Jacob as El Shadday, but I didn't make myself known to them by my name Yahweh.

Exodus 6:2-3 (NOG)

𝕬ppendix

YAHWEH

"He is the eternal, independent and self-existent Being: He is the Being whose purposes and actions spring from within, without foreign motive or influence:

He is absolute in dominion; He is the most pure, the most spiritual of all essences;

He is infinitely benevolent, infinitely beneficent, infinitely true, and infinitely holy;

He is the cause of all being, the upholder of all things;

He is immeasurably happy, exceedingly perfect, without any finite or measurable limits; and eternally self-sufficient, needing nothing that He has made:

He is illimitable in His immensity, inconceivable in His mode of existence, and indescribable in His essence;

He is known fully only to HIMSELF, because an infinite mind can be fully apprehended only by itself.

This unknown God that Paul was declaring to the Athenians is the Being who, from HIS infinite wisdom, cannot slip up, make mistake or be deceived; and who, from His infinite goodness, can do nothing but what is eternally just, right and kind." This unknown God is now made known to you. His name is YAHWEH ELOHIM! Hallelujah!

For my unsaved friends, let me tell you today that Yahweh doesn't have to remain unknown to you. He has a purpose for your life. If you hear His voice today, do not harden your hearts. Remember that while you are in transit on earth, God winks at the times of your ignorance but now you have heard me declare this unknown God to you today and encourage you to repent.

My friend, seek ye the Lord while He may be found, call upon Him while He is near. If you are wicked, turn from your ways…if you are unrighteous, let God control your thoughts. Return to God. He is merciful, He will have mercy upon you and justify you…. Make you pure as if you have never sinned.

What more could you ask for! What a God! Do you know Him? Do you want to know Him? The choice is yours! Will you pray this prayer right where you are, right now?

PRAYER

Dear Jesus, I believe that you are Lord and Saviour of the world. I believe that you will forgive me of my sins and make me righteous, so I now confess that I am a sinner and ask that you forgive me of my sins and trespasses. Thank you for dying for my sins. Help me to walk in newness of life and to boldly proclaim that

YHWH is the eternal God. I ask this in Jesus' name.

Amen.

Exodus 6: 2-8 Names Of God Bible (NOG)

[2] *Elohim* spoke to Moses, "I am *Yahweh*.

[3] I appeared to Abraham, Isaac, and Jacob as *El Shadday*, but I didn't make myself known to them by my name, *Yahweh*.

[4] I even made a promise to give them Canaan, the land where they lived as foreigners.

[5] Now I have heard the groaning of the Israelites, whom the Egyptians hold in slavery, and I have remembered my promise.

[6] "Tell the Israelites, 'I am *Yahweh*. I will bring you out from under the oppression of the Egyptians, and I will free you from slavery. I will rescue you with my powerful arm and with mighty acts of judgment.

[7] Then I will make you my people, and I will be your *Elohim*. You will know that I am *Yahweh* your *Elohim*, who brought you out from under the forced labor of the Egyptians.

[8] I will bring you to the land I solemnly swore to give to Abraham, Isaac, and Jacob. I will give it to you as your own possession. I am *Yahweh*.'"

BIBLIOGRAPHY

Ancient-Greece. "History of the Acropolis"
        http://ancient-greece.org/history/acropolis.html (Accessed
February 24, 2015).

Ancient Greece. "Epicurus" 2003-2012 University Press Inc.
        www.ancientgreece.com/s/People/Epicurus (Accessed April 7,
2015).

Andrew Wommack Ministries. Teaching God's Unconditional Love &
Grace, Acts 17:18. http://www.awmi.net/bible/act_17_18 (Date accessed
July 4, 2015).

Bible Study Manuals. "Jewish Marriage Customs"
        http://www.biblestudymanuals.net/jewish_marriage_customs.htm
(Accessed March 16, 2015).

Biblehub. http://biblehub.com/commentaries/acts/17-16.htm (Accessed
February 17, 2015).

Connolly, Peter. *Ancient Greece.* Oxford University Press, 2001.

Dake's Annotated Reference Bible: Containing the Old and New
Testaments of the Authorized or King James Version Text. By Finis
Jennings Dake. Lawrenceville, Georgia: Dake Publishing Inc., 2010. Print

Diamant, Anita and Howard Cooper. *Living A Jewish Life.* New York:
Harper Collins Publishers, 1991

Fisher, Leonard Everett. *The Olympians Great Gods and Goddesses of
Ancient Greece.* New York, NY: Holiday House, 1984.

Gundry, Robert H. *Commentary On The New Testament.* Massachusetts:
Hendrickson Publishers Marketing, LLC, 2010.

Hawthorne, Leroy. "God's Biblical Calendar – Yahweh Elohim" Bible
Studies. Bible Truth Church of God International, Bronx, NY 2009

Honderich, Ted. *The Oxford Companion to Philosophy.* Oxford New York: Oxford University Press.

Hurlbut, Jesse Lyman. *The Story of the Christian Church.* Zondervan Publishing House, 1970.

Jewish Virtual Library "Judaism; Who Is A Jew" www.jewishvirtuallibrary.org (Accessed April 28, 2015).

Macdonald, Fiona. *Gods & Goddesses In The Daily Life Of The Ancient Greeks.* Columbus, OH: McGraw-Hill Children's Publishing, 2002.

Morrison, Martha A. and Stephen F. Brown. *Judaism World Religions.* New York: Infobase Publishing, 2006.

Nelson's NKJV Study Bible. USA: Thomas Nelson Publishers 1982.

New English Translation (NET) Bible. Biblical Studies Press, L.L.C. 2005.

Parker, Steve. Aristotle and Scientific Thought. Chelsea House Publishers, 1995.

"Phaenomena, Translated by G.R. Mair", http://www.theoi.com/Text/AratusPhaenomena.html (Accessed February 2, 2015).

Rees, Rosemary. *Understanding People In The Past; The Ancient Greeks.* Crystal Lake, IL: Heinemann Library, 1997.

Simowitz, Gene R. *Evangelism: A Road Less Traveled.* Xulon Press, 2012.

Tarsus, Turkey, http://www.sacred-destinations.com/turkey/tarsus (Accessed February 7, 2015).

ABOUT THE AUTHOR

Dr. Monica Dennis-Jones gave her life to the Lord at the tender age of 9. Born to Mr. & Mrs. Joubert Dennis in the district of Kendal, Hanover, Jamaica, she is the first of five children for her parents. She migrated to the United States of America where her involvement in church ministry expanded and blossomed. She was appointed an Evangelist by Bishop Leroy Hawthorne, of the Bible Truth Church of God International, in New York.

Desiring to adequately equip herself for spiritual ministry and developing people, Dr. Monica (as she is affectionately called) pursued an Associate Degree in Theology; a Bachelor's Degree in Theology; a Master's Degree in Pastoral Counseling and a Doctoral Degree in Theology, graduating Suma Cum Laude. Soon after, she pursued her second Doctorate degree, Doctor of Philosophy in Pastoral Ministry; and a third Doctorate degree, Doctor of Education Specialization in Christian Education.

Dr. Monica Dennis-Jones is a talented leader, coach, conference speaker and organizer who enjoys singing, playing the guitar, cooking, traveling and a good game of football (soccer). She hosts the radio programs, Karibbean Prayze; Beautiful Day; The Night Watch; Karibbean Konnection and Island Hopping aired on Caribbean Gospel Radio FM.

*In 1997, Dr. Monica married Franklyn Jones and the union produced two children, Kennedy and Kendra. Dr. Monica seeks to please Yahweh in every area of her life. Her motto is **"I determine who I will be today. Since it is my choice, I choose to be my best, give my best and do my best."***

The contents of this publication were submitted to Newburgh Theological Seminary as a Dissertation for my 2nd Doctoral Degree, Ph.D in Pastoral Ministry in 2015.

"Dissertation is approved.

Overall good content, organization and Bibliography.

Strong information and useful in ministry and

surely was helpful to you in your study and preparation."

Congratulations

Newburgh Seminary staff